FARM MONOPOLY GATES COUPLE TO DIVORCE

18 CATTLE FARMERS AND RANCHER ORGANIZATIONS WANT RELIEF PROMISED BY USMCA AGREEMENT!

"The Meat Issue"

2016 **Hillary Rodham Clinton** VP presidential running mate consideration **BILL GATES IS THE OWNER OF THE LARGEST FARMLANDS IN AMERICA**. Gates has invested in meat alternative products, such as BK's "**Impossible Burger**" and the plant-based "*Beyond*" burger.

Bill Gates believes cows are contributing to greenhouse gases and "GLOBAL WARM - ING" by the cattle supposedly "EXHALING" 6% of the methane gas in the atmosphere. Melinda French Gates started talking with divorce lawyers in 2019 after news became public of Bill's ties with the convicted sex offender **Jeffrey Epstein. Gates and Epstein met multiple times between 2011 and 2014,** according to *The New York Times*, *The Wall Street Journal*, and *The New Yorker*... **Melinda French Gates wants no alimony but will be entitled to half** (50%) **of Bill's $130 BILLION** (USD) **fortune.** Bill's Private-Public Partnership (PPP) with the Communist People's Republic of CHINA (and work in China since 2007) should help him weather the storm. **Zhe Shelly Wang**, Bill Gates' Asian interpreter **denies an affair.** The retreat where Bill Gates and his ex-girlfriend, **Ann Winblad**, spent long weekends together even after he got married is available for rent. **BIG81 – KBHB** is South Dakota's ONLY ranch station featuring extensive coverage of livestock, commodity, and financial markets world news with *ABC News*. Our late grandparents, dad and uncles were ALL farmers.

SYNTHETIC MEAT?

Synthetic meat investor Bill Gates calls for rich countries to shift entirely to synthetic meat...Mr Gates, who has invested in a range of 'synthetic meat' startups made the comments in an interview promoting his new book '*How to Avoid a Climate Disaster*'. Bill Gates reportedly owns 242,000 acres (about a third of the size of Rhode Island) of farmland across as many as 18 states—with the biggest holdings in Louisiana and Arkansas... The farmland is technically owned by separate entities indirectly tied to the Gates, through a company called Cascade Investment. "A spokesman for Cascade Investment declined to comment on any of the details associated with these transactions or the Gateses' holdings, other than to say that Cascade is very supportive of sustainable farming," journalist Eric O'Keefe wrote. "*Beef demand is everything... Prosperity of all beef industry participants hinges critically upon consumer demand,*" says Ted Schroeder, noted agricultural economist and director of the Center for Risk Management at Kansas State University. "*Every new dollar that enters the industry comes from the consumer...*". **Now you understand that it is the world's 4th richest man** ($130B USD; soon to be 17th richest divorced man) **behind the "CANCEL CULTURE CAMPAIGN" against America's National Cattlemen's Beef Association, butcher shops, mom & pop family farmers and the 18 rancher and livestock organizations in the USA.**

Dec., 24, 1935- 2021

ON MY PLATE
PUBLISHER'S
NOTE & PART

It's one year later after consumers were told to Stay Home. Save Lives… In this issue, we spring forward with articles geared towards getting back out there to barbecue, dine more, cook and fellowship at church and at home—as we support local gourmet food and lifestyle businesses — especially our mom & pop restaurants!

My Creole and military veteran mom, **Sheila Ellen Long**, passed away on February 3, 2021. This past year many others have lost family and friends to coronavirus—as well as accidental deaths, disease, **HATE CRIMES**, natural causes and suicide. I recently visited a friend whose wife committed suicide while he was working at home—sad!

Mom was the director of the **City Mission Bible Club** in the 1970s and '80s—and sent many kids to Bible camp at **Camp Pattersonville**. She also volunteered at **SCAP**, while dad worked at General Electric (GE)…Our parents were married 39 years—dad passed away in 2008. In recent years, up until undergoing back-to-back brain surgeries, after falling in a downtown restaurant, mom was part of the **Jay St Drum Circle**. After her surgeries she retired to Florida, where she experienced a stroke, and came back to Schenectady for Hospice care. I sat by mom's bed the last months of her life and watched her slowly die… **What does all that have to do with "Spring Forward"?** Well, the answer to that question is the theme of this issue of *Taste of Schenectady®*, which is **PERSEVERANCE through faith and trust in God!**

Schenectady's Jay Street and *The Open Door Book Store* is where I first shopped as a teenager… That was over forty (40) years ago that my late mom and her friend, the late **Karen B. Johnson**, allowed us kids to walk around the corner from our parish at St. John The Baptist to Jay Street. **Our mom loved shopping downtown Schenectady** at the cheese cake store, the *Planter's Peanuts Shop* and *Woolworth's* department store.

In the 1980s, my friend, Frank, his grandma, and I, operated a pizza parlor and Italian ristorante on State Street, in downtown Schenectady, near to Proctors.

In the last few years, **The Dilly Bean** has opened on Jay Street, the **Clinton Street Mercantile** around the corner, **Schenectady Trading Company** opened on lower Union Street — and **Arthur's Market** reopened in March 2021 — all these businesses sell locally made products. At these stores — as well as at the **Hungry Chicken Country Store**, located in Rotterdam Junction, you will find some food and locally made crafts. The *Niskayuna Food Co-Op* is the **ONLY REAL food Co-Op** in Schenectady County… Indeed, our parents instilled in us a passion for **the arts**, **crafts** and **gastronomy**—*the art and science of good eating*… In this issue, we spotlight three (3) artisanal delis in the area—*Dnipro Euro Foods*, *Gershon's Deli & Catering*, and *Sal's Quality Market*… Sal's is one of the best butcher shops in the area… Also, check out our spotlight on *The Big Body Butcher* and its certified Japanese Wagyu beef… Speaking of Asian-inspired foods, *Bonchon Chicken & Cajun Seafood* recently opened on upper Union St — seafood boil combo deals.

It's time to get back out there and support farmer's markets, as well as BBQ, picnic, and plant your garden—and *Buhrmaster Farms* has mulch, screened organic compost, garden soil, and topsoil for delivery or pick-up. Maybe it's time to take your car in for service, or time to buy a new car. If so, head over to *Metro Ford*, on upper State Street for sales, service, collision work and parts.

Frank Gallo Florist delivers 7 days a week if you are looking for that special arrangement to show you care.

Check out our article on planning the perfect picnic for you and your partner, and the travel stories in this issue.

Cinco de Mayo, **Mother's Day**, and **Father's Day** remind us that spring is a time of celebration and joy! And, we have hacked a recipe for the Mexican dish *Al Pastor* — that is perfect for caterers, cooks, food truck owners, and outdoor festival pitmasters to prepare on a roasting spit.

THE AMERICAN SPIRIT IS ALWAYS ABOUT PERSEVERANCE THROUGH FAITH AND TRUST IN GOD — AND NOT JUST ON MEMORIAL DAY, VETERANS DAY AND THE 4TH OF JULY!

If you are reading this publisher's note, I'll remind you that we cannot take credit for the fact that we are still alive when over 500,000 Americans have died due to coronavirus. **We cannot take the credit for our PERSEVERANCE** — so love God, love your family and ALL people — and cook, dine and shop responsibly!

Let this issue encourage and inspire you, your family and friends — share it with others. Lastly, thanks for reading *Taste of Schenectady®* and *Beyond*™ magazine — *The Gourmet Food, Lifestyle and Travel Connection©*

of schenectady®

tasteofschenectady.com

PO Box 293 · Schenectady, NY 12305
(518) 831-0534

David J. Long, Jr., CDM, CFPP, KOFC
Publisher and Editor-in Chief

Contributors
Amada Walsh, Jessica Diaz, Fran Schmidt,
John Williams, Lillian Peterson, Tony Gomez,
Melissa Hart, Pamela Wayne, Amy Simpson

CONTENTS

Sal's Quality Market

4 BBQ & Grill — four generations of quality meats and more!

Gershon's Deli—67 Years!

8 The deli & catering tradition continues with Tony's daughters

A Taste of Dnipro Euro

12 European gourmet flavors from the Baltic to the Black Sea

Caribbean & Hispanic

18 Where to buy and what to buy and what to cook to enjoy Street Food

East Coast Destinations

20 Discovering new and beautiful places surrounded by leisure and nature.

Buhrmaster Farms

35 Spring and summer gardening tips, compost, mulch, topsoil and more!

Sal's Quality Market

A Family Business Since 1900

Four Generations of Quality Meats & More!

Sal's Quality Market is a locally owned and operated shop with a large selection of fresh meats, deli, heat & serve entrées, and home made Italian sausage.

Beef, Chicken Sausage, Pork Butt, Ribs, Steaks
BBQ & Grill Meat Packs

Also, check out our weekly specials and fliers

Sal's Sausage & Peppers $35

A Full Line of Poultry Products

Sal's Heat and Serve Entrees

Chicken Parm	$45.
Eggplant Parm.	35.
Meat Lasagna	35.
Veggie Lasagna	35.
Baked Ziti	32.
Meatballs	36.
Sausage & Peppers	35.
Cavatelli with Broccoli	35.
Tossed Salad	20.
Antipasta Salad	30.

All Serve 8-10 People
Please Give 48 hour notice

Sal's QUALITY MARKET

CALL IN YOUR ORDER
518-346-0408
2713 Guilderland Ave. (RT158)
Schenectady, NY 12306
www.SalsMarket.com

Call In Your Order!
(518) 346-0408

2713 Guilderland Ave
Schenectady, NY 12306

Prices and availability subject to change.

 SalsQualityMarket   **salsmarket.com**   @SalsMarket

In 1900 Antonio Sindoni started a grocery and meat market on Broadway in Schenectady. Six years later his son Salvatore was born and eventually he was working at his father's market. Over the years Sal owned a number of businesses, but eventually he opened a small grocery shop in Rotterdam, New York, just like his father. In 1943 he named that business **Sal's Quality Market.** Sal's son William Sindoni grew up working at the age of

10 in his dad's business, just like his father. In 1977, he bought the business to concentrate more on meats. William operated the business with the help of his wife Jo, his sons Michael and Thomas, and nephew Jim, until his passing at the ripe age of 80.

William "Bill" Sindoni
Nov. 10 1940 – Mar. 12, 2021

Sal's Quality Market still offers the best choice of butcher shop bargains through its fourth generation — and they make their own retail store line of gourmet fresh kielbasa, Italian sausages—and gourmet breakfast links.

Today, when you walk into Sal's Quality Market, you will find the freshest cut meats, poultry, produce, frozen cut veggies, pastas, sauces, spices — and of course a full delicatessen of cheeses, meats and salads… If you are planning a backyard BBQ, graduation party, picnic, or simply like to grill, go to **Sal's Quality Market** at 2713 Guilderland Avenue!

BBQ, GRILL & SMOKER PACKS

BEEF, BURGER, VEAL, STEAKS

Sal's Grill Pack *4 lb Country Style Pork Spareribs,* **$69.95**
2 lb Lean Ground Chuck Patties, 2 Whole Fresh Chickens,

3 lb White Eagle Skinless Hotdogs, 3 lb Sal's Italian Sausage Patties

Sal's Super Pack *3 lb Sal's Link Italian Sausage,* **$124.9**

5 lb Country Style Pork Spareribs, 3 lb Lean Center Cut Pork Chops,
3 lb Boneless Pork Shoulder Roast — Great for Pulled Pork!

3 lb Boneless Sirloin Steaks, 3 lb Extra Lean Rump Roast,

3 lb Lean Ground Chuck, 2 lb Extra Lean Stew Beef,

1 Whole Fresh Chicken • **WE CAN SCHEDULE CURBSIDE PICK-UP!**

I shop at Sal's Quality Market for most of my meats. I buy their beef, pork and veal meatloaf blend for meatloaf—and veal cutlets to make Caponata, Piccata and Veal Saltimbocca—and fresh sausage and rolls when I want to simply grill and make grinders. Sal's Quality Market fresh made kielbasa, flank steak, marinated half-chicken and butcher-tied pork butt are ALL perfect for the BBQ and Grill!

If you want the best bargains at a local butcher, you've got to go shop at Sal's Quality Market! ADV.

PLAN A PERFECT PARTNER PICNIC

Getaway ideas for you and your significant other

By Amanda Walsh

A perfect picnic should not require too much planning and thought, which if overdone can be tiresome. Instead, think about the memories you wish to make together. A simple, quiet evening in a park or a field, away from the noise and clutter of urban living, can leave you with experiences that last a lifetime.

Here are some picnic ideas for you and your sweetheart:

The Beach:

Might sound clichéd, but a walk on a beach in the cool summer breeze at dusk is one of the most pleasurable experiences you can have with your partner.

If you don't live in a coastal area, perhaps you can book a short vacation. Laze around, sun bathe, collect shells, build sandcastles, and take a walk as the waves wash over your feet and sun sets in the background. **Albany, Schenectady and Troy are home to a vast array of attractions that appeal to all ages!** From amusement parks and river cruises to hotspots just for kids and spectator sports, discover the abundance of attractions the Capital Region has to offer.

State Parks and Hiking Trails:

Discovering new and beautiful places surrounded by nature is a divine adventure. Sharing these moments with your partner adds to the experience, and will leave you with beautiful memories of the sun peeping through the canopies and wildflowers that grow on the foot of tall mossy trees. The **Mohawk-Hudson Bike Hike Trail** provides recreation for all to enjoy. The path is open to all for bicycling, walking, running, and inline skating. **Riverside Park** in the Stockade is a perfect picnic place!

Historical Places and Ruins:

There is just a natural romantic aura around old mansions, castles, forts, temples, and other architectural sites. Perhaps it's the feeling of being out of time that creates these sensations. Making history together can be the theme of your date if you and your partner enjoy scenic architecture.

Museums and Art Galleries: If your partner enjoys art and artifacts, surprise them with tickets and trips to museums that have been on their list to visit. Exploring art together is sure to be a bonding experience — once all local museums reopen to the public.

Plan a Road trip: A road trip is a versatile idea that can vary according to your convenience. Long drives give you the opportunity to talk, unwind and enjoy the weather. What's romance if not that?

A peaceful car ride along a straight highway with just you and your loved one can be a great chance to talk, share old memories and make new ones.

Do you wish to plan the perfect picnic getaway and are looking for romantic picnic ideas? Contact any of the **gourmet shops** and **delicatessens** in this issue of *Taste of Schenectady*® and *Beyond*™ magazine now.

www.frankgallo.com

Daily Delivery

**throughout the Capital District
7 days a week**

*Serving the Capital District
since 1920*

Contact us at
518.346.6171

frankgallo.com

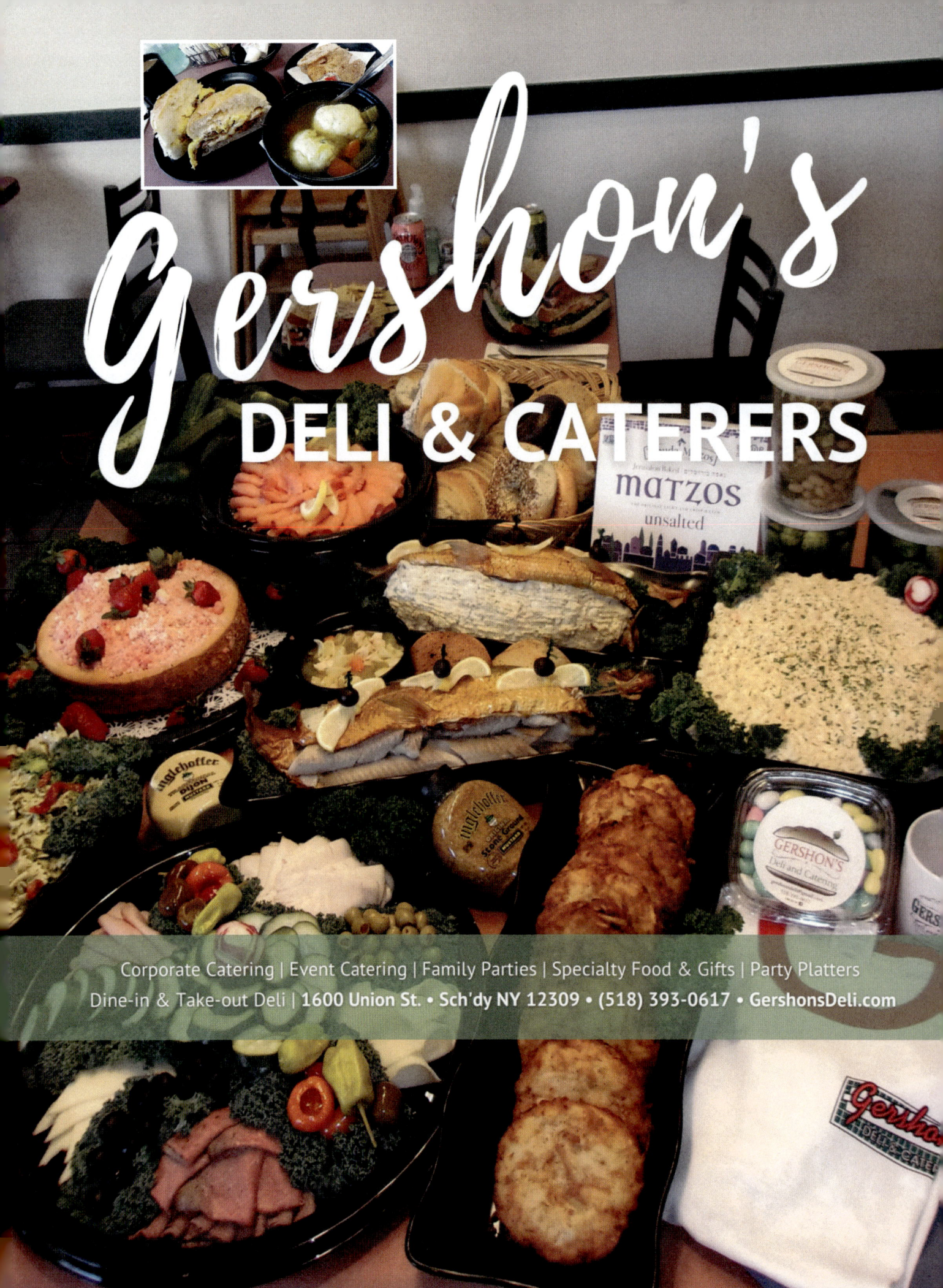

Gershon's
DELI & CATERERS

Corporate Catering | Event Catering | Family Parties | Specialty Food & Gifts | Party Platters
Dine-in & Take-out Deli | **1600 Union St.** • Sch'dy NY 12309 • **(518) 393-0617** • GershonsDeli.com

Gershon's Deli & Caterers

1600 Union St.
Schenectady, NY 12309
(518) 393-0617

- Breakfast and Lunch
- Catering & Deli
- Specialty Foods & Gifts
- Order Pick-up
- Order Delivery

www.gershons.com

Gershon's Deli is still a family-owned catering company and delicatessen — celebrating 67 years!

Once upon a time, the word, "deli" was short for "kosher delicatessen," a restaurant that specialized in the cured meats and hearty fare of a Jewish immigrant community. Today, **Gershon's Deli & Caterers** still offer **corned beef**, **brisket**, **pastrami**, **turkey**, **gourmet entrées**, **salads**, **smoked fish**, **soups**, and **desserts**, and much more! It all started in 1954, when Irv and Lena Gershon opened their deli. They quickly outgrew their original store and in 1956, moved across Union Street to the present-day location. Over the course of two decades, the Gershon's Deli name spread throughout the region, along with a thriving catering service. In 1973, **Antonio "Tony" Lauria** (born 1954 in Sicily), immigrated at the age of 19 to the United States looking for work. That same year, Irv and Lena sold Gershon's Deli to their nephew Bob Lessner.. In 1978, Tony Lauria became a counterman and cook at Gershon's Deli. Tony Lauria purchased Gershon's Deli from Lessner, who referred to him as his "adopted son," in 1985... For the next 31 years with his business partner Lou Gregory (who retired in 2009), Tony Lauria presided over this legendary eatery, until his passing away on September 9, 2016. Next, Tony's daughter, **Antonia "Toni" Nelson**, took over the business... She and her sister inherited **Gershon's Deli** — open Monday-Wed 7-3 • Thur-Friday 7-6 • Sat 7-5 (Sunday catering only). At Gershon's Deli they take great pride in **catering office lunches and corporate events** — and catering family **Bar/Bat Mitzvahs**, **anniversaries**, **bridal and baby showers**, **birthday parties** and other special occasions.

Whether you're looking to feed a crowd or having an intimate gathering of family and friends, let Gershon's Deli & Caterers help you plan your next event. At home or in the office, Gershon's always earns rave reviews for its signature platters, beef and chicken entrées, pasta dishes, appetizers and world famous desserts. From soup to nuts and everything in between, Gershon's Deli & Caterers make every occasion delicious! **For catering call Gershon's Deli!**

ADV.

BREAKFAST & UMAMI

FYI: On April 26, 2021, Digital *Condé Nast* magazine *Epicurious* published an article claiming that it "*will no longer publish recipes featuring beef*"… It actually enacted this policy in 2019 and **has published beef recipes** since then. *Epicurious*' **new sponsor is Lightlife Foods**, a company that produces plant-based foods.

NOTE: None of the **Top 10 restaurants** in this editorial feature are paid advertisers / sponsors.

f @tasteofschdy #tasteofschenectady

BACON, BISON, WAGYU, AND WILD BOAR GOURMET BURGERS

By John Williams

This writer loves trying burgers and bacon sandwiches from lively food joints from around the Capital region!

Nothing appeases a meat lover's appetite than a juicy, meaty and bodacious burger stacked with bacon, and dripping with cheese and sauces! Bursting with umami, deep, and sharp flavors, burgers take your taste buds on a journey! They are so popular that over 50 billion burgers are consumed in America every year. An American eats one burger every three days on average. Burgers come in all shapes, sizes, and types. Here are some of the top picks of meats to make gourmet burgers by *Taste of Schenectady®*:

BACON

Fried to crispy, fatty perfection makes bacon exquisite on its own. But you add it to an already incredible cheeseburger and you have something simply divine!

Food & Travel Editor David Long recently visited the *Hungry Chicken Country Store*, located in Rotterdam Junction, for their *Widow Maker* breakfast sandwich. The egg and bacon-filled breakfast sandwich also comes with grilled heavenly ham and sizzling sausage on a bun. Our editor heard about the *Hungry Chicken Country Store* after speaking to the folks at *Dave's Gourmet Burgers*, which reopened at 16 Edison Avenue in downtown Schenectady. Before heading out to the country store, he stopped at *Arthur's Market* to shop at the re-opened Historic Stockade (1795 est.) coffeehouse and restored neighborhood market (*see photo upper left*).

BISON

Bison is gaining popularity as a top choice of meat for burgers. Bison is not commercially raised but is usually grass-fed, which means it is full of nutrients and vitamins such as the B-12, selenium, and zinc. Grass-fed animals also have higher levels of omega-3s, and bison has the same level of omega-3s as salmon. *Dave's Gourmet Burgers* offers **3 Bison Burgers**—one was voted #1 in the entire Capital region in 2015! Game meat makes a great burger. **Dave's Gourmet Burgers offers exotic burgers**, such as; Alligator, Camel, Elk, Kangaroo, Ostrich, Lamb, Python, Rabbit, Wild Boar, etc., and Kobe beef burgers.

* **BILL GATES IS THE OWNER OF THE LARGEST FARMLAND IN AMERICA...** Bill Gates believes cows are contributing to GLOBAL WARMING. He has invested in a range of 'synthetic meat' startups, such as BK's "Impossible Burger". **Synthetic meat investor Bill Gates calls for rich countries to shift entirely to synthetic meat**, which he wrote in his book, '*How to Avoid a Climate Disaster*'. Now you understand that it is the world's 4th richest (soon to be 17th richest/divorced) man behind the **"CANCEL CULTURE CAMPAIGN"** against America's eighteen (18) cattle farmer and ranch associations.

WAGYU

Wagyu was introduced by Japanese cattle breeders that bred European and Asian cattle together. Wagyu meat has remarkable fat marbling, spread evenly throughout the meat instead of clumping up in giant white patches. This gives it a distinctly pink color instead of red.

The fat in Wagyu beef melts at extremely low temperatures, even lower than your body temperature. It quite literally melts in your mouth, leaving you with an unmatchable umami flavor... **See our feature on Wagyu available at The Big Body Butcher on page 32**.

WILD BOAR

Wild Boar is low in calories — compared to pork butt it is higher in protein. Wild boar tastes like a cross between pork and beef. Wild boar meat is a bit darker due to its high iron content. It is sweet and nutty as wild boars eat nuts from the forest. **Beef / MEAT burgers are here to stay!**

Wild boars are the go-to choice for people looking for healthier lifestyles. Previously thought to be a specialty beef, it is quickly gaining popularity and becoming increasingly common on upscale restaurant menus.

All gourmet burgers deserve love and appreciation... Every kind of meat has its own charm. However, the ones listed here are your gateway to burger heaven.

Here's a shortlist of the **Best Burger Joints** rated by foodies — **we've been checking on them to guarantee quality and update the list** — tell them *Taste of Schenectady* sent you:

1. **Dave's Gourmet Burgers** • 16 Edison Ave • Sch'dy
2. **20 North Broadway** • 20 N Broadway • Sch'dy
3. **Build A Burger Pub** • 2012 Central Ave • Albany
4. **Maxon's American Grill** • 507 Saratoga Rd • Glenville
5. **Wagon Train BBQ** • 671 Mariaville Rd • Sch'dy
6. **O'Toole's Restaurant** • 1814 Central Ave • Colonie
7. **The Horses Lounge** • 912 McClellan St • Sch'dy

   On Feb. 19, 2021, Fred Fritzen passed away. He had turned over the biz to his son, "Lil Fred" who moved back to Sch'dy in 2014.

8. **Mohawk Taproom** • 153 Mohawk Avenue • Scotia
9. **Katie O'Byrne's** • 121 Wall St • Sch'dy
10. **Druthers Brewing Co** • 221 Harborside Dr • Sch'dy

A Taste of
DNIPRO

BY FOOD & TRAVEL EDITOR
DAVID J. LONG, JR., CDM, CFPP

GOURMET FLAVORS FROM THE BALTIC TO THE BLACK SEA

Twenty-one years ago, a Ukrainian smart man decided to leave what today is known as **Dnipro** — formerly known as *Dnipropetrovsk* but renamed during the process of de-communization after the most recent uprisings. Today, Dnipro is an industrial center of Ukraine that was a hub for the Soviet military industry. As such, no foreigners were allowed to visit Dnipropetrovsk without official permission until the 1990s. So, this expat decided to open **Dnipro Euro Deli**, in Latham, New York, six-years-ago, to share his love and passion for the Ukrainian food of his former homeland — and other Eastern European imported gourmet foods.

Dnipro Euro Deli is a family owned and local delicatessen with a sensational selection of Eastern European food such as German, Polish, Ukrainian and Russian-style fresh cut, cured and smoked fish, meats and prepared foods. The store stocks over seventy (70) items that also include European butters, confectionaries, imported breads, fresh made salads, a variety of pierogi, potato pancakes, oven-ready prepared foods, groceries, frozen entrées, Italian deli meats, sauces, soups — and **stuffed turnovers with savory meat fillings**.

Dnipro Euro Deli has a large selection of caviars, cheese — domestic and imported — and a large inventory of organic products, Non-GMO and preservative free foods…

Dnipro Euro Deli also caters to individuals with special dietary requirements and take-out catering.

When you walk into Dnipro Euro Deli, the Ukrainian and Polish-language magazines and newspapers in the foyer — the plethora of charcuterie choices — Euro breads on a board — as well as all the aisles and shelves stocked with marinated and pickled salads — all beckon your senses and tantalize your tastebuds. I first stumbled across Dnipro Euro Deli a year or so ago while surfing the internet for purveyors nearby that sold imported and sustainable caviars.

On our first trip and culinary tour of Dnipro Euro Deli, we bought **Ajvar** (Serbian roasted red pepper sauce) that we served straight out of the jar and smeared on **fried fillets of smelts** that we purchased — along with **sprats**, **pork liver pâte**, pickled cucumber salad, Bavarian **Landjaeger** ("Land Hunter") sausage, **Polish clabossy** (smoked kielbasa), a dozen **pierogis**, **Suillus** marinated mushrooms in the jar, four ounces of bulk **Ukrainian-Russian bulk red sturgeon caviar**, **Icelandic cod liver** — and a tantalizing triangle-shaped loaf of authentic **Vollkornbrot** (German whole-grain bread, that's nutrient dense with a fabulous texture and positively packed with flavor)!

BTW: **Dnipro Euro Foods imports its Eastern European artisan breads directly from Germany** par-baked and frozen — and then finishes baking the breads on the premises — before displaying the assorted whole loafs for sale in the store…

NOTE: *If you wish to store European deli foods, remove the products from the deli wrap and keep in a tight container (see left top photo). This will allow the meat to breathe and not sweat inside the plastic, keeping the meat fresher for longer.*

By Executive Chef David Long

The Grill and Outdoor Smoker Kitchen with Sal's Quality Market Meats

Applewood branches kept this low and slow smoldering smoke infusing these foods prepared with love, and passion!

All we did was add a little kosher salt to **Sal's Market marinated half chicken** before smoking it with *Hungry Chicken Country Store* **applewood**. We pre-seasoned Sal's **flank steak** with *East to West Coast Spice* "**Ultimate Spice**" and added kosher salt to the meat — it came out truly scrumptious!

Sal's Quality Market fresh made **kielbasa** we perfectly smoked as-is and served it with grilled **long hot peppers** and smoked onions. In the photo here you can see the spices that we used to dry Rub Sal's **pork butt**... After 1 hour of smoking, I basted the pork for 6 hours with apple cider vinegar mixed with EVOO and the leftover rub. At *Arthur's Market* we bought **Lovin' Mama Farm** kale micro-greens and **fresh mozzarella** — we smoked the fresh mozzarella cheese in cheesecloth — and smoked porcini mushrooms and **San Marzano Organic Tomatoes**. We **Pickled red onions** and grilled deli rolls to make huge crostini — dat's truly an outdoor home kitchen serving **Cucina Italiana Rustica!**

AFTERNOON TEA IN THE 21ST CENTURY

It's Time for Exotic Iced Teas, Kombucha and Tasty Treats!

By Lillian Peterson with Editor's Note Disclaimer

While classic English afternoon tea still has its charm and sophistication, exotic iced tea, kombucha, and other sweet, iced drinks give it a fun, 21st-century twist!

Iced Tea

Feel fancy with a glass of iced tea topped with a lime wedge as you relax under the spring and summer sun and bathe in its warmth. Doesn't that sound exquisite? You might be a coffee lover but trust us when we say that if you try iced tea once, you will never wish to go back.

Iced tea comes in many flavors. Bigelow oil has a citrusy profile and undertone, which is found in Earl Grey and can easily be made at home. Thai tea is infused with the richness of spices. Cardamom, cloves, and cinnamon? Sign me up!

Kombucha

This healthy probiotic drink has a tangy twist and is healthy for your body. You can brew kombucha in your home with a little bit of practice.

Kombucha cleans up your digestive tract and restores healthy bacteria in your gut. This has numerous health benefits — and you can flavor your kombucha with some healthy fruits, ginger, berries, or lime. Play around with flavor profiles until you find your personal favorite. Also, many gourmet shops sell brewed kombucha from dispensers, and refill bulk bottles.

Iced Watermelon Basil Matcha

The name itself sounds delightfully regal. This matcha blends watermelon and basil to produce the most refreshing drinks that are fit for a spring and/or summer day. This red and green, visually pleasing tea will surely make you fall in love with iced teas. **EDITOR'S NOTE:** *I love coffee and espresso drinks* (.) *Lillian loves tea* (lol).

Why enjoy tea instead of other beverages

• Tea has numerous benefits. Here is why we think iced tea is a much healthier choice than coffee:

• It keeps you hydrated. Even more so than hot tea. After water, it is the second-best source of hydration!

Iced teas are rich in antioxidants and a healthier alternative to soda.

• Iced tea will strengthen your bones and boost your metabolism with high magnesium content. Tea may have a calming effect and help reduce anxiety and stress.

• Tea also has dietary flavonoids that reduce the effects of aging such as wrinkles and help your skin protect itself against sunlight.

There are numerous benefits of drinking tea. Discover tea globally with *Taste of Schenectady*® and *Beyond*™ magazine — by visiting our advertisers and non-paid retail shops on **p. 30-31**.

WE'VE GOT AMBITION FOR WHATEVER!

For twenty-one (21) years, Ambition Bistro and Nott Street Office have served Schenectady County with the most creative cuisine, copies and office supplies. Through Greg and Marc you'll experience the difference!

People ask, "What do you do?" I respond, "Whatever it takes!"

Our dining room and fully stocked bar are reopened and available for dining-in. Visit our barista, who prepares our espresso-based coffee drinks, smoothies and teas — or stop in for just for take-out. **Each day, foodies feed on Ambition Bistro!**

We specialize in serving breakfast and specialty sandwiches Monday through Friday 8am till 3pm, and a phenomenal Brunch— that many patrons purchase daily as pick-up.

At Ambition Bistro Build-Your-Own Salad all-year-long. The salad selections are as eclectic as the specialty sandwiches — and the crisp, fresh greens and fresh vegetable garnishes make the perfect accompaniment and/or entrée.

154 Jay St. · Schenectady · Call (518) 382-9277

ambitionbistro.com

Rely on **Nott Street Office** for the technology and services you need to get the job done… We offer all your **shipping and packing needs** under one roof… We have state-of the-art digital copiers for optimum copy quality and speed. **No copy or print job too small or too big.**

2215 Nott Street · Niskayuna, NY 12309 · Call (518) 382-2663

nottstreetoffice.com

Nott Street Office — Around the Block …Around the World

CARIBBEAN AND HISPANIC MARKETS

WHERE TO BUY AND WHAT TO COOK TO ENJOY STREET FOOD

By Jessica Diaz and Executive Chef (retired) David J. Long, Jr., CDM, CFPP

We, at *Taste of Schenectady*, believe that food is one of the core parts of a culture, and Hispanic culture is diverse with a mixture of influences from various regions. From the ethnic fresh specialty cuts of pork to the style of cooking, Caribbean and Hispanic cuisine are delectable, unforgettable and one-of-a-kind. And, if you are like us, you will butcher your own pork belly to make **carnitas** and/or shop at many different butchers to make ethnic foods. We do get take-out at **Mami's** restaurant on Crane St, and **San Francisco Restaurant**, Albany St; and **Roy's Caribbean Restaurant**, State St — all in Schenectady.

What is 'Hispanic' Cuisine?

The U.S. Census Bureau classifies the term "Hispanic" as referring to the region, and not the race of people. It uses the term to describe any person, regardless of race, creed, or color, whose origins are Mexican, Puerto Rican, Cuban, Central or South American. These recipes reflect our Latin and Creole decent (Caribbean, English, French, Italian, and Spanish). **Creole and Latino people** seem more apt to appreciate diverse cuisine and the cultural influences on cooking-styles. People in Louisiana embrace Creole culture.

Some of our favorite foods include chayote, plantains (green and extra ripe sweet varieties), pork and cassava aka yucca root. After rice, yuca is one of the most popular sources of carbs in Caribbean and Hispanic meals. Lately, our chef has been collecting dried chili peppers typically used in Mexican and **Mestizo** cooking… **Al Pastor** ("Shepherd-style) is an achiote (annatto seed) paste, Mexican oregano, and rehydrated dried chili, EVOO, garlic, spices, and pureed vegetable marinated pork dish — that is cooked on a vertical BBQ spit. . Similar to the Greek **Gyro** (lamb layered with pork fat) meats and Middle Eastern **lamb Shawarma** cooked on a spit, *Al Pastor* was brought to Mexico by Lebanese immigrants. Mexican TV chef Patricia Jinich of *Pati's Mexican Table* makes *Al Pastor* by sautéing the marinated pork in a pan on the stove… Our chef and team were inspired to cook and hack this Mexican "**STREET FOOD**" dish to inspire festival and home cooks, chefs, and food truck owners.

Where to Buy Ethnic Equipment and Ingredients?

Caribbean and Hispanic markets are the places to buy authentic, ethnically sourced ingredients and cookware that will provide the original taste and bona fide experience. However, we could not find a vertical roasting spit, so our chef went to the Home Depot® store and bought a carbon steel masonry pointed stake and paving stone for $7.15 combined… Thanks to the guys at Home Depot in the tool rental area, who drilled a hole in the paving stone, so we could build our "**Al Pastor vertical roasting spit**".

AL PASTOR RUB: Toast and grind: 1 T allspice berries, 1 T cinnamon sticks, 1/4 C annatto, 1 T cumin, 1 T coriander, 1 tsp mustard seeds, and 1 tsp melange peppercorns. Remove the bone from a pork butt, slice off the fat cap and save, and cut the pork into 1/2 inch thick slices — season with the Rub. **MARINADE:** In a kettle, heat 1C EVOO to 350° F and flash-fry: 3 Ancho, 3 Guajillo and 3 Pasilla chili peppers. Cool and remove the stems and seeds. Blend the chilis with 2 C chicken stock, 7 garlic cloves, 3 scallions, 1/2 C fresh cilantro with stems and 2 fresh squeezed oranges, 1 lime juiced, 1 C fresh pineapple, and 1 Tb EVOO in a blender. Pour over the pork and marinate 3 hours. **Recipes continued on pages 25-26.**

Recipes continued on pages 25-26.

TOP 10 EAST COAST TRAVEL DESTINATIONS

By Amy Simpson

CAMPGROUND RESORTS

Campgrounds are the most appealing rest sites for an adventurous time at the beach. It allows convenient access to golden sand, scenic views, and cool blue water. The East Coast hosts numerous campground sites and resorts snuggly placed right next to the warm sand.

Here are the top four (4) campgrounds on the East Coast of our choice:

Assateague Island State Park in Berlin, Maryland is the state's only oceanfront park with unimaginable vistas at your disposal.

The **Beverly Beach Camptown** in Florida is a year-round camping destination and has various activities to keep everyone busy on its 1,500-foot linear beachfront.

Myrtle Beach State Park in South Carolina is known as the Golf Capital of the World. It is famous for its endless golf courses for people of every age and offers affordable camping stays.

The **Hither Hills State Park** in New York 122 miles away from NYC and is perfect for surfing.

BNB INNS

If you are more of an inn person and don't fancy RVs or camps, don't worry, we've got you covered! Bed and Breakfast inns are quickly gaining popularity as one of the most comfortable yet affordable choices for vacations.

Here are three (3) of our favorite cheap BNB Inns on the East Coast for your consideration:

Firefly Bed & Breakfast in Lincoln, Vermont is priced at less than $100 for two rooms for a night. It also comes with a delicious, full breakfast. Wake up to a scenic view with a beautiful park!

The Wilderness Inn Bed & Breakfast is perfect for nature lovers who like to be surrounded by greenery. It is a lodge-style BNB in New Hampshire's White Mountain National Forest. During off-peak times, you can afford rooms for less than $100.

The 1785 Inn in North Conway, New Hampshire is the perfect holiday getaway! The cheap package make for an ideal family vacation.

TIMESHARES

If you're looking for cheap Timeshares on the East Coast, we have three (3) picks for you:

Sheraton Vistana Resort Villas give you a chance to stay at luxurious suites right near Disney. There's even a pool to dip your toes into!

Beach Quarters Resort in Virginia has an oceanfront and offers various sports and an indoor pool for those beach vacation feels!

Westgate Lakes Resort in Orlando, Florida is a luxurious timeshare resort perfect for the entire family. It includes an exquisite water park with numerous pools, a spa, a mini golf course, and various sports courts. It's also at a convenient distance from world-famous theme parks.

There are numerous affordable travel destinations on the east coast, discover great getaways with *Taste of Schenectady*® and *Beyond*™ magazine!

1 IN 3 ADULTS HAS PREDIABETES.
COULD BE YOU, YOUR DOG WALKER, YOUR CAT JOGGER.

WITH EARLY DIAGNOSIS, PREDIABETES CAN BE REVERSED. TAKE THE RISK TEST.

DoIHavePrediabetes.org

ad COUNCIL   AMA AMERICAN MEDICAL ASSOCIATION   CDC CENTERS FOR DISEASE CONTROL AND PREVENTION

> However without an island, the cooks, are still facing away from the activities while cooking."

Common Kitchen layouts and remodelling designs

Kitchen layouts include the one-wall kitchen, the galley kitchen, the U-shaped kitchen, the G-shaped kitchen, and the L-shaped kitchen   **By Kitchens.com**

Deciding on a layout for a kitchen is probably the most important part of kitchen design. It's the layout of the kitchen—and not its color or its style—that determines how easy it is to cook, eat and socialize in the kitchen. At the most basic level, the layout addresses the placement of the appliances, the sink(s), the cabinets, the counters, the windows and doors, and furniture such as a kitchen table and chairs.

If you're remodeling, the structure of the existing home will limit the options. The most common kitchen layouts include the one-wall kitchen, the galley kitchen, the U-shaped kitchen, the G-shaped kitchen, and the L-shaped kitchen—some of which can also incorporate an island.

Like the one-wall and galley floor plans, a U-shaped layout is an efficient kitchen designed for one primary cook. Basically a wide galley kitchen with one end closed off, it keeps onlookers out of the main work area while remaining open to other rooms of the home and allowing traffic to pass.

Problems with the traditional U-shaped kitchen typically arise due to its small size. For one, it doesn't offer room for a kitchen table and chairs. Secondly, depending on where the sink is situated, it may be impossible to fit the dishwasher right next to it.

With the increase in great rooms and loft-style living and the decline of the formal dining room, open floor plans and

L-shaped kitchens have become very popular. As you would expect, this layout consists of two adjacent, perpendicular walls. It can range in size from small to large, depending on the length of the legs—but without a dividing wall between the kitchen and living area, the legs could be long indeed.

People who like to entertain will appreciate this layout's ability to incorporate multiple cooks, invite guests into the cooking area and allow for mingling and conversation during a family dinner or a cocktail party. However, without an island, the cooks are still facing away from the activities while working. To turn the room into an eat-in kitchen, you'll probably want a good old-fashioned table and chairs. The best part about that: Unlike most islands with seating on just one side (what some designers compare to "frogs on a log"), everyone can face each other throughout the meal. Besides, the tabletop can be used as a work surface, too.

If you're thinking about changing the layout of your home kitchen, make sure to call a bona fide kitchen remodeler. Make sure to spends time discussing your design plans.

COOKING GADGETS AND HOME KITCHEN TRENDS

New Gadgets for Home Cooks and DIY Kitchen Design • By Fran Schmidt

Do you love cooking with the latest and coolest culinary tools? Let's talk about cooking gadgets that will improve your cooking experience even more:

Silicone Strainer

The silicone strainer is designed to clip onto pots or bowls of any size for easy and safe straining. This gadget allows you to strain without having to lift and pour the food out of the pot. It is practical, time-efficient, and dishwasher safe.

Stainless Steel Straws

Trying to go green? Buy a pack of stainless-steel straws and a straw cleaner to reduce plastic waste and help save the environment. These straws are dishwasher safe, economically friendly, and trendy.

Anti-Fatigue Mats

It is tiring to work all day in the kitchen, especially during the holidays. The anti-fatigue mask can be placed under your feet to provide comfort to your legs and feet.

Stainless Steel Odor Absorber

Working in the kitchen often means that your hands will smell when handling onion, garlic, meat, or any other smelly ingredient. Stainless Steel bars are shaped like soap and they help absorb any odor from your hands, leaving them smelling fresh.

2020-2021 has seen a drastic change in the modern home kitchen design trends. Here are some popular trends to look out for:

Popping Colors

Kitchens are no longer monotonous and chrome. Popping colors is an emerging trend which people are accepting with open arms. Pick a color that makes you happy and paint a wall, the kitchen island or cabinets for a fresh look.

Going Handle-less

Cabinet handles can be a pain to deal with in the kitchen, especially when your apron or clothes keep getting stuck as you prance around conjuring up dishes. Modern designs allow innovative press-open cabinets and recessed handles for a handle-less, practical kitchen.

Gold Finishes and Veiny Marbles

Both trends are the mark of true luxury in the modern kitchen. Veiny marbles went out of style as white synthetic countertops took their place. But now, marbles are back in the game. They are sustainable, durable, and timeless.

With these kitchen gadgets and design trends, give the heart of your home a welcome makeover!

WE HACKED AL PASTOR BY BUILDING OUR OWN ROASTING SPIT

All it took was a little creativity and a trip to our local home building supply store to "stakeout" this recipe!

By Jessica Diaz and Executive Chef (retired) David J. Long, Jr. (Continued from page 18)

While the **Al Pastor** meat marinates at room temperature for 3 hours, it is time to get your grill and smoker ready.

EQUIPMENT: Chimney charcoal starter, newspaper, applewood chunks soaked in hot water, grill lighter, large cast iron pan to hold the paver brick with the hole and an 18-inch high carbon steel pointed stake with 3 inches cut off from the flat end of the masonry stake, and pineapple.

ASSEMBLY AND COOKING METHOD:

The Lebanese that brought Al Pastor to Mexico knew as many cultures do, that there is beauty to spit-roasting meat. As the pork spins and slowly cooks, the robust fat drippings from the meat trickle down, helping to baste the pork beneath it. Watching the crispy exterior of the cooked, deep-red meat is mesmerizing. Many restaurants buy cooked gyro meat to heat, slice, and serve. However using our pointed stake and paver stone spit-roaster you just layer the fat and marinated meat by pushing it down the stake and over a 2 inch cut round pineapple base.

We used indirect smoke heat and closed the grill lid to cook the pork on the spit at 275° F for 6 hours—turning the pan with oven mitts every 30 minutes. If you like your Al Pastor crispy on the outside, place it over hot coals or in a 375° F oven for another 30 minutes. Before slicing the pork vertically, let the Al Pastor rest for 20 minutes—and serve with fresh grilled homemade tortillas and/or store bought griddled **Street Taco** tortillas, diced onion, diced scallion, diced fresh grilled pineapple, and salsa verde. **FYI: You can substitute boneless lamb**.

HOT TAMALES MADE WITH SPIT–ROASTED AL PASTOR PORK

Thin slices of Al Pastor pork bring a sweet heat to this Mexican traditional favorite made with Maseca!

By Jessica Diaz and Executive Chef (retired) David J. Long, Jr.

MASECA is the Gluten Free leading global brand of corn flour — that is fortified with vitamins and minerals — it adds an earthiness to these fun to make purses of masa, pork and veggies — known as **Tamales Al Pastor**.

TAMALE DOUGH:

3 C Maseca corn flour

2 ½ C warm water or low-sodium chicken stock

1tsp salt • 1C lard

In a mixer combine the Maseca, salt, lard and water and mix until a dough forms. Allow the dough to rest.

ASSEMBLY AND FILLING:

Banana leaves, cut into squares large enough to fill

Masa Dough made from scratch at room temp

Al Pastor marinated cooked pork slices, Al Pastor sauce, chopped cilantro, scallions, tomatoes and sliced tomatillo, kernel corn, dice onion & pineapple

Fold the diced cilantro, scallion, tomatoes, onion and pineapple into the dough. Place a scoop of dough mixture on the center of each banana leaf. Place some of the Al Pastor pork slices on the dough, and drape with some of the sauce, followed by a tomatillo slice. Roll each banana leaf around the filling and fold the ends over to seal the purses. Tie each tamale with butcher twine. Simmer the tamales in low sodium chicken stock for 12 to 15 minutes in batches. **Serve one or two Tamales Al Pastor per person…Open, eat and enjoy with butter** (optional).

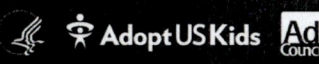

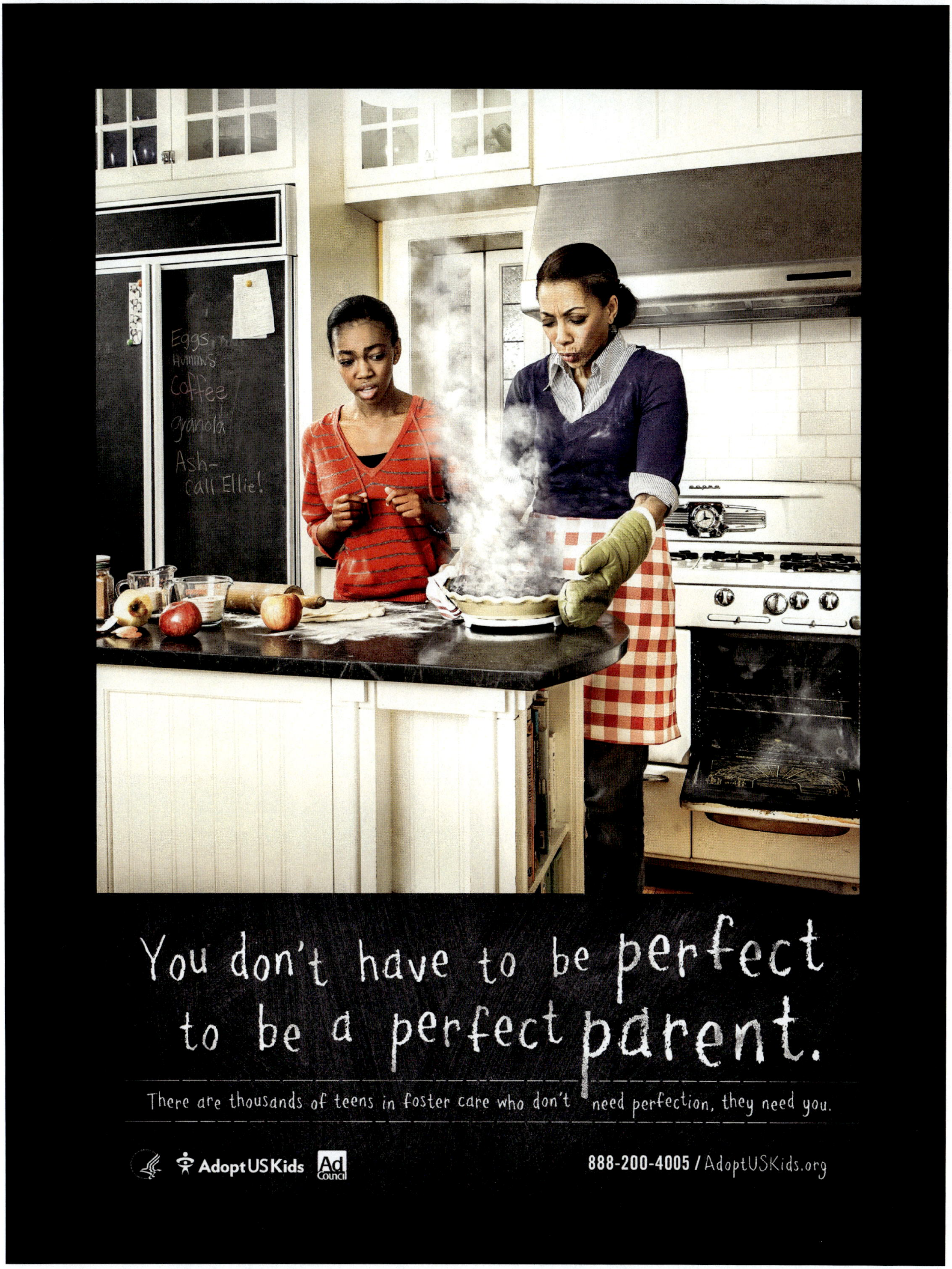
Eggs
Hummus
Coffee
granola
Ash–
call Ellie!
You don't have to be perfect
to be a perfect parent.
There are thousands of teens in foster care who don't need perfection, they need you.
AdoptUSKids
Ad Council
888-200-4005 / AdoptUSKids.org

Best Places

BUFFALO WINGS

By Melissa Hart

The crispy skin that crumbles as you bite down enhanced by the spicy, tangy sauce that drenches your lips, and bursts Buffalo wings provide a divine sensory experience unlike any other. Buffalo wings are a heartthrob in New York's dining scene for a reason.

Do you plan on traveling this season and want to dine out on authentic Buffalo wings in the place that made this pub food famous? If so, here are the top three (3) picks for wings in Buffalo, New York by *Taste of Schenectady*® and *Beyond*™ magazine:

Gabriel's Gate

No one does wings like Gabriel's Gate. Their wings have a perfect balance of creaminess, tanginess, and spice. Each wing is fried to perfection. They know how to get the frying just right. The skin is not tough or chewy; it is crisp and fatty and produces a satisfying crunch when you bite. The half-cabin half-bar aura of **Gabriel's Gate** is unique and appealing to visitors, further enhancing your wing-eating experience.

Elmo's Restaurant and Sports Bar

Elmo's double-dip chicken wings are unparalleled and a local favorite. They know their sauce game like Tom Brady knows football. Their crispy and tender wings have taken people by a storm, especially since they have been a runner-up in the *Chicken Wing Tournament* that *Buffalo Eats* holds.

Beyond Buffalo — Duff's or Young's Wings?

Duff's Famous Wings is becoming a popular tourist destination. Duff offers all levels of spice to fit people's varying preferences. **Did Teressa Bellissimo actually invent Buffalo Wings?** A newspaper article published about her family's **Anchor Bar** during 1969 does not mention their Buffalo wings, but Duff's, began selling Buffalo wings in that year. **In 2013, Buffalo finally recognized John Young, who moved to Buffalo from Alabama in 1948,** and began serving uncut chicken wings that were breaded, deep fried and served in his own special tomato based *"Mumbo Sauce"* at his Buffalo restaurant, beginning in 1961. Young stated that the **Anchor Bar didn't offer Buffalo wings as a regular menu** item until 1974. He registered the name of his restaurant, **John Young's Wings 'n Things**, at the county courthouse before leaving the Buffalo area in 1970.

THE ANNUAL SCHENECTADY

WING WALK IS IN OCTOBER...

Each year, the Wing Walk normally attracts thousands of visitors to Downtown Schenectady on the first Saturday of October. In 2020, the DSIC, explained, "Due to social distancing guidelines and limitations on public gatherings surrounding the COVID-19 pandemic, we were unable to organize the usual Wing Walk as we have for the past eight years." **Area restaurants instead sold wing packages for pick-up.**

f @tasteofschdy #tasteofschenectady

DUFF'S WINGS

Best local ETHNIC BITES

●●●●●

Chicken & Cajun Seafood

Bonchon Wings, Fried Fish, Fried Shrimp, Chicken or Seafood Fried Rice, Crawfish, Mussels, Snow Crab & Seafood Combos come with Corn, Egg, Potato and Sausage!

Union Bonchon Chicken/Seafood 1638 Union St (518) 901-0033

●●●●●

Curry, Jamaican Jerk & More

Scrumptious Jerk Wings are to die for! Curry Chicken, Jerk Chicken, Oxtail, Escovitche, and Jamaican Beef/Chicken Patties, and more... When we don't want to cook it, we go here!

Roy's Caribbean · 769 State St. Sch'dy, NY (518) 346-1677

●●●●●

Really Good Spanish food

If you want to experience Puerto Rican and Domincan food at its best, you've got to go to this place before 1pm most days. Really cheap eats with a lot of variety!

San Francisco · 872 Albany St Sch'dy NY (518) 382-5962

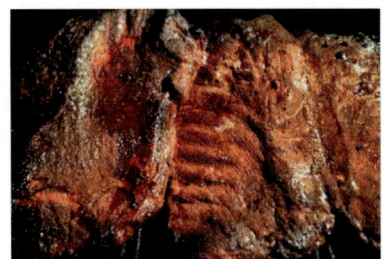

●●●●●

Best BBQ and Smokehouse

The best BBQ and smoked meats in the area! The burnt ends, ribs, pulled pork & chicken are luscious and sure to please! These guys are artisanal BBQ experts.

Memphis King · 1902 Van Vranken Ave (518) 372-5464

●●●●●

Best Italian Family-Style

For appetizers, banquets, catering, dinner, and desserts, Ferrari's Ristorante provides authentic Italian food with a passion for high quality authentic cuisine.

Ferrari's · 1245 Congress St Sch'dy, NY (518) 382-8865

●●●●●

Best Kosher-style Deli

Huge sandwiches, like corned beef and pastrami, are served at this Jewish-style deli. Breakfast, Lunch and Dinner entrées. Gershon's caters all special occasions.

Gershon's Deli · 1600 Union Niskayuna (518) 393-0617

●●●●●

Best Butcher and Italian Deli

Sal's Quality Market is a locally owned and operated shop with a large selection of fresh cut meats, deli, home made Italian sausage and grocery staples!

Sal's Mkt · 2713 Guilderland Ave Sch'dy ·NY (518) 346-0408

●●●●●

Best Eastern European Food

Dnipro Euro Deli is a family owned and local delicatessen with a delicious range of Eastern European food imported from Ukraine, Russia, Poland, and Germany.

Dnipro Euro · 898 Loudon Rd Latham NY (518) 213-7007

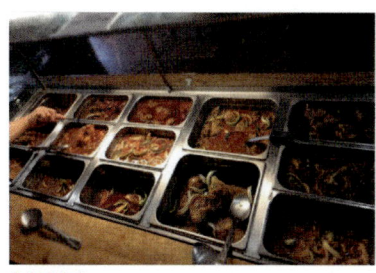

●●●●●

Puerto Rican & Dominican

Enjoy a taste of authentic Puerto Rican and Dominican food from Mami's hot food steam table—it's not a buffet—it's yummy entrées served a la carte with sides!

Mami's · 911 Crane Street Sch'dy NY (518) 377-8700

GOURMET SHOPS AND SPECIALTY STORES

FISH & SEAFOOD MARKETS

Anker's Fish House
420 Altamont Ave • Schenectady, NY
(518) 382-8842

Combos Fish Fry
865 Crane St. • Schenectady, NY
(518) 377-6636

Fin Your Fishmonger
2050 Western Ave • Guilderland, NY
(518) 452-4565

The Fresh Market
664 New Loudon Rd • Latham, NY
(518) 786-5150

ETHNIC MARKETS

Asian Market
1245 Central Avenue • Albany, NY
(518) 438-8886

Parivar Spice & Indian Food
1275 Central Ave • Colonie, NY
(518) 512-5118

Timothy's World-Ramesh West Indian Mkt
820 Crane St • Sch'dy NY
(518) 372-2332

1028 State St. • Schenectady, NY
(518) 346-8802

BUTCHERS & FAMILY MARKETS

Aladdin Halal Market
309 Central Avenue • Albany, NY
(518) 443-1001

Avon Market
1631 VanVanken Ave • Schenectady, NY
(518) 374-3197

Buckley Farm
946 Saratoga Road • Rt. 50
Ballston Lake (518) 280-3562

Dnipro Euro Foods
898 Loudon Rd • Latham, NY 12110
(518) 213-7007

Fred The Butcher
1473 U.S. 9, Clifton Park, NY
(518) 371-5333

Gabriel's Supermarkets
255 Mohawk Ave
Scotia, NY
(518) 370-0140

1924 Curry Rd
Rotterdam, NY
(518) 355-2230

Niskayuna Food Co-Op
2227 Nott St
Schenectady, NY
(518) 374-1362

Predel's Ranch
59 Garnsey Rd
Rexford, NY (518) 399-0265

Rolf's Pork Store
70 Lexington Ave • Albany, NY
(518) 463-0185

Sal's Quality Market
2713 Guilderland Ave • Schenectady, NY
(518) 346-0408

Sahr's Cash & Carry
2068 Curry Rd, Schenectady, NY
(518) 355-2210

The Big Body Butcher
2008 Central Ave • Colonie, NY 12205
Across from The Costumer (518) 414-3260

COFFEE, TEA , JUICE BAR & MORE

Ambition Bistro
154 Jay St • Schenectady, NY
(518) 382-9277

Apostrophe Café
432 State St • Schenectady, NY
(518) 881-4515

Arthur's Market & Café
35 N Ferry St • Schenectady, NY
(518) 709-0019

Bellevue Café
2630 Broadway• Schenectady, NY
(518) 393-7720

Broadway Lunch
2101 Broadway • Schenectady, NY
(518) 372-3222

Bud's on Jay Street
185 Jay St • Schenectady, NY
(518) 952-4466

Lili Rita's Café
432 Franklin Street • Schenectady, NY
(617) 939-8877

Raw Juice & Smoothie Bar
177 Jay Street • Schenectady, NY
(518) 707-6680

Storied Coffee
109 Mohawk Ave • Scotia, NY 12302
(518) 387-3210

Takes_Two Café
433 State Street • Schenectady, NY
(518) 280-9670

BAKED GOODS AND MORE

Bagels and Bakes
1927 Curry Rd • Schenectady, NY
(518) 355-6801

Bella Napoli Bakery
672 New Loudon Rd • Latham, NY
518-783-0196

721 River Street • Troy, NY 518-274-8277

Cappiello Foods
510 Broadway • Schenectady, NY
(518) 370-0860

Capri Imports Italian Deli
2617 Broadway • Schenectady, NY
(518) 346-6511

Civitello's Italian Pastry Shoppe
42 N Jay Street • Schenectady, NY
(518) 381-6165

Gershon's Deli & Bakery
1600 Union St. • Schenectady, NY
(518) 393-0617

Full Belly Deli & Bakery
2601 Guilderland Ave, Schenectady, NY
(518) 280-5272

La Gioia Deli
2003 Van Vranken Ave • Schenectady, NY
(518) 372-2949

Perreca's Bakery & Gourmet Shop
33 W. Jay St • Schenectady, NY
Sch'dy (518) 372-1875

Villa Italia Bakery
226 Broadway • Schenectady, NY
Schenectady (518) 355-1144

GOURMET SHOP • IRSH FOODS • PASTA • SAUCE

The Dilly Bean
133 Jay Street • Schenectady, NY
(518) 894-7911

Lennon's Irish Shop
164 Jay Street • Schenectady, NY
(518) 377-0064

Pede Brother's Pasta
582 Duanesburg Rd • Schenectady, NY
(518) 356-3042

Casa Visco Sauces
819 Kings Rd, Schenectady, NY
(518) 377-8814

COOKBOOKS • HOME • KITCHENWARE SUPPLY

Different Drummer Kitchen Supply
1475 Western Ave • Albany, NY 12203
(518) 459-7990

Spoon & Whisk • 1675 U.S. 9
Clifton Park, NY (518) 371-4450

Habitat For Humanity
115 Broadway • Schenectady, NY
(518) 395-3412

Made in The Stockade
Wood Cutting and Charcuterie Boards
(518) 434-3334

Open Door Bookstore
128 Jay Street • Schenectady, NY
(518) 346-2719

Clinton Street Mercantile
148 Clinton St • Schenectady, NY 12305
Sch'dy • (518) 280-8580

The Schenectady Trading Company
609 Union St • Schenectady, NY 12305
(518) 280-3036

Sign-up for a chance to WIN A FREE COOKBOOK on our website

FARM STANDS AND COUNTRY STORES

Brown's Family Farm Stand
1174 Fort Hunter Rd
Schenectady, NY 12303
(518) 836-4806 • Firewood in Season

Buhrmaster Farms
189 Saratoga Rd • Scotia, NY 12302
(518) 399-5931

Fo'Castle Farm Country Store
166 Kingsley Rd
Burnt Hills, NY 12027
(518) 399-8322

Hungry Chicken Country Store
Rotterdam Junction
661 River Rd #6505
Schenectady, NY 12306
(518) 879-9442

Lakeside Farms
336 Schauber Rd
Ballston Lake, NY 12019
(518) 399-8359

CANDY • CHOCOLATE • NUTS • GOURMET POPCORN

Bittersweet Candy
173 Jay Street • Scotia, NY 12302
(518) 280-6061

Krause's Homemade Candy
1609 Central Ave • Albany, NY 12205
(518) 869-3950

**Uncle Sam's All-American
Chocolate Factory**
2571 Albany Street • Schenectady, NY
(518) 372-2243

What's Poppin Albany
Kohl's Plaza
1814 Central Ave • Albany, NY 12205
(518) 704-3936

SPICES • OILS • VINEGARS

East To West Spice Company
16 Edison Street • Schenectady, NY 12306
(518) 918-7870

Oliva! Gourmet Olive Oils & Vinegars
Stuyvesant Plaza
1475 Western Ave • Albany, NY 12203
(518) 482-3866

Penzeys Spices
Stuyvesant Plaza
1475 Western Ave • Albany, NY 12203
(518) 650-8364

Testa's Pantry • Balsamics & Olive Oils
600 Franklin Street • Suite 104
Schenectady, NY 12305
(518) 669-3755

FLORISTS

Frank Gallo & Son Florist
1599 State St • Schenectady, NY
(518) 399-2424

1790 Altamont Ave • Rotterdam, NY
(518) 356-1111

WINE, BEER & SPIRITS

Annand Wine & Liquor
1437 Broadway • Schenectady, NY
(518) 374-8329

Boscia's Liquor Discount
2710 Broadway • Bellevue
Schenectady, NY
(518) 346-5706

Capital Wine
348 State & Lark Streets
Albany, NY (518) 689-0160

Eastern Wine Liquor
1619 Eastern Pkwy
Schenectady, NY (518) 346-8085

Englebardt's Wine & Liquor
511 Union St • Schenectady, NY
(518) 372-4788

Freemans Bridge Wine & Liquor
100 Freemans Bridge Rd
Scotia, NY
(518) 688-0789

Glenville Beverage
96 Freemans Bridge Rd
Scotia, NY
(518) 374-4615

Goosehill Wine & Liquor
1529 Van Vranken Avenue
Schenectady, NY (518) 357-3545

Great Flats Brewing Company
151 Lafayette Street
Schenectady, NY (518) 280-0232

King Cork Wine & Liquor
2430 Watt St • Schenectady, NY
(518) 393-3955

Mad Jack Brewing Company
237 Union Street
Schenectady, NY (518) 348-7999

Madison Wines & Spirits
795 Madison Ave • Albany, NY
(518) 455-9463

Sabatino Liquor
210 Quail Street • Albany, NY
(518) 462-4411

Scotia Wines & Spirits
25 Mohawk Ave • Scotia, NY
(518) 346-1872

Ferreira-Carpenter Estates
Try our variety of family made wines
For wholesale inquires call:
(518) 598-4854

"I worked at lots of restaurants and kitchens of all kinds. I later discovered that my specialty is Gourmet Burgers," says Chef Dave Khan... At East to West Spice Company their mission is to bring seasonings to your kitchen. The company as well as **Dave's Gourmet Burgers** reopened on April 12th — along with their new gourmet shop at 16 Edison Avenue — off Broadway —in downtown Schenectady, NY.

**EAST TO WEST SPICE COMPANY
(518) 918-7870**

WAGYU BEEF

A TASTE OF JAPAN AND MORE AT
THE BIG BODY BUTCHER

When consumers hear the term Kobe, the first thought that comes to mind is typically not a city in Japan, but rather a juicy steak right off the grill…Wagyu beef is globally renowned for its rich flavor, juiciness, and tenderness and high marbling content.

A *Taste of Schenectady*® and *Beyond*™ Gourmet Spotlight

Hokkaido Snow Rib-Eye (above) • Kobe Wine Filet Mignon

Highly prized for its rich flavor, Wagyu beef is among the finest gourmet beef in the world. Wagyu is any of the four Japanese breeds of beef cattle… In Japan cattle are classified and raised by prefecture such as Kagoshima, Hyogo, Miyazaki and Hokkaido… **Japan's Kobe Wagyu beef** is type of Wagyu globally renowned for its high marbling content, juiciness, rich flavor and tenderness… At **The Big Body Butcher**, in Colonie, NY, their mission is to supply gourmet food aficionados with the highest quality meat for the best price! Owner/Butcher Cody Shields has over 10 years of experience and started butchering back in 2007. Shields founded **The Big Body Butcher** in October 2018, after working as a head butcher and general manager for several butcher shops. He continues to supply foodies all over the country with the most sought after meats and game.

There are four different breeds of Wagyu cattle: Japanese Black, Japanese Brown, Japanese Shorthorn, and Japanese Polled. Japanese Black cattle comprise about 90% of the Wagyu cattle breeds… **The Big Body Butcher imports 100% certified Wagyu beef directly to its store from Japan** — as well as imports Wagyu from Australia. The Big Body Butcher supplies American Wagyu as well as Japanese Wagyu. Japan's well sought-after 100% certified Wagyu beef cuts guarantee that the Wagyu was farm raised by prefecture and packaged in that specific geographical zone and according to tradition. Consider this your **comprehensive guide** to the exquisite qualities of the cuts of 100% certified Japanese

Wagyu beef that The Big Body Butcher offers. To start off, Japan's Hokkaido island is the most northern region, resulting in much lower temperatures than the rest of the country. **Hokkaido** gets its name "Snow" from the marbling on the steaks making it almost white! It is some of the rarest Wagyu in the entire world and deservingly so! Its extremely rich and robust with flavor!

Hokkaido Snow NY Strip $200 lb ($150/12oz)
Hokkaido Snow Rib-Eye $200 lb ($150/12oz)

Japanese Black cattle from **Kagoshima** Prefecture are marketed under the brand name "Kagoshima (Black) Beef". **Kagoshima NY Strip** cost $150 lb ($112.50/12oz);

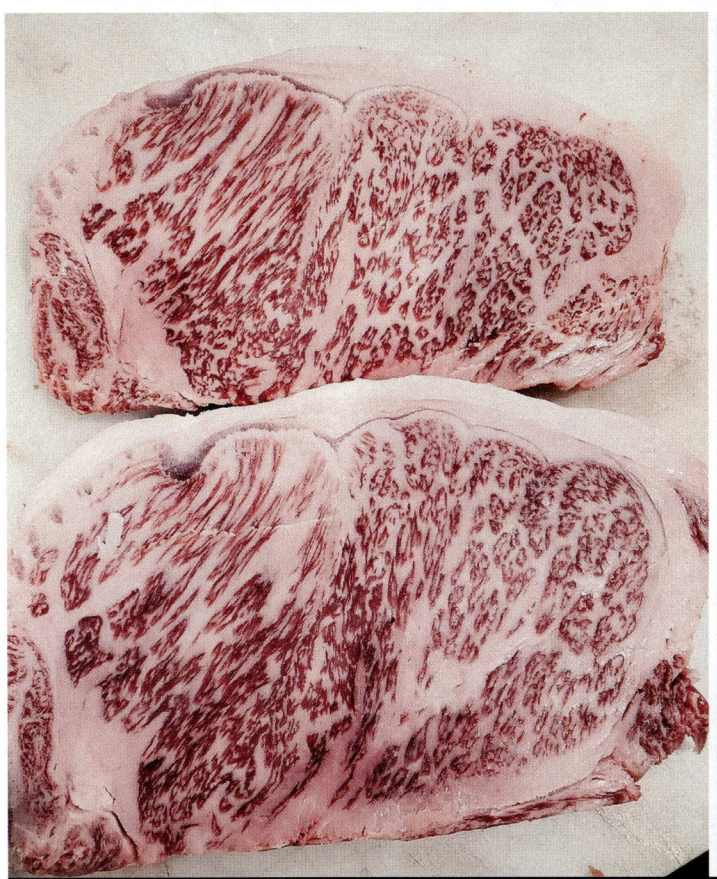

Kagoshima NY Strip (above) • Kobe Wine Rib-Eye

Miyazaki Filet Mignon

Kagoshima Rib-Eye $150 ($112.50/12oz); **Kagoshima Filet Mignon** $200 ($100/8oz).

Kobe beef is a very particular strain of Wagyu called Tajima-Gyu that is raised to strict standards in the prefecture of Hyogo. Hyogo's capital city is Kobe, thus the name. **Kobe Wine** is an incredibly tender cut generating a sweet buttery flavor. A crowd-pleasing cut, Kobe Wine is easy to cook. Japanese farmers mix in just the right amount of fermented grapes (wine) into the cattle feed to give the Wagyu a flavor profile unlike any other! **Kobe Wine NY Strip** cost $200 lb ($150/12oz); **Kobe Wine Rib-Eye** $200 ($150/12oz); **Kobe Wine Filet Mignon** $225 ($112.50/8oz).

Miyazaki is one of the top brands of Japanese Wagyu beef known for its quality and consistency. Produced from Japanese Black cattle, and raised in Miyazaki prefecture, it has become known for its snowflake-like marbling. In order to qualify as Miyazaki Wagyu beef, cattle must be born and raised in Miyazaki Prefecture in Japan, and graded A4 and above. Miyazaki has won the "Wagyu Olympics" in 2007 and 2012 which is the first time in the history of the tournament that a Japanese brand has been able to win consecutive awards. **Miyazaki NY Strip** cost $150 lb ($112.50/12oz); and **Miyazaki Rib-Eye** cost $150 lb ($112.50/12oz)

The Big Body Butcher recommends a 12-16oz cut of Miyazaki rib-eye, but will accommodate your desired weight over 12 ounces. **Miyazaki Filet Mignon** $250 ($125 / 8oz)…A 6-8oz cut of the Miyazaki filet mignon is recommended.

For questions about any products, or help with placing your order, don't hesitate to contact The Big Body Butcher by phone: (518) 414-3260… The shop is located at 2008 Central Ave, Albany NY 12205— in the same parking lot behind Men's Inc barber shop and *Every Days Build A Burger* restaurant (across the street from *The Costumer* store). ADV

Our paternal grandparents, **Louisa Washington (Johnson)** and **Thomas Long**, migrated from Culpeper, Virginia circa 1912 to Hopewell Junction, NY, and later opened the **Long farm** and **Johnson CSA farm** by 1933 in Poughkeepsie. Over the past three decades, **Community Supported Agriculture (CSA)** has become a popular way for community members to buy organic, seasonal food directly from a local farm.

BUHRMASTER FARMS...
SPRING INTO GARDENING & MORE!

For well over 50 years, Buhrmaster Farms has been fully committed to offering the freshest local fruit, produce, and more! They provide **garden plants** and premium **landscaping mulch**—including red mulch, black mulch, cedar mulch, bark mulch, **screened organic compost**, **garden soil** and **topsoil** for delivery or pick-up.

One of the easiest ways to prepare your outdoor space is to add a fresh layer of mulch to garden beds. Mulch helps the soil retain moisture for your flowers and plants, and keeps down weeds. It often takes more mulch than people expect to cover a flower bed... Newly planted perennials need time to grow new roots before the hot summer weather sets in. **Summer bulbs**, such as alliums, agapanthus and cannas, should be planted in spring, when the soil is beginning to warm up... Make sure to add fresh mulch around all your new plants. Shop here for perennials and summer annuals to plant at home.

COMMUNITY SUPPORTED AGRICULTURE (CSA)

Buhrmaster Farms' Community Supported Agriculture (CSA) works with you: The farm issues (sells) "shares" of their crop to the community. As your investment matures, you reap dividends in the form of a basket of fresh produce each week! **Here's an example of a "Full Share":** **A Share** entitles the customer to a weekly harvest of fresh produce — a full range of vegetables, herbs, and small fruit (berries). A **Fruit Share** includes tree fruits such as peaches, plums, cherries, pears, and apples. The season runs June through October and their produce is available as harvested. Your shares will be provided in a half bushel basket. **Pick up day for the CSA program** is Thursday, between 1 pm to 6:30pm. *Pick Your Own Flowers* at the farm stand starts in July...Please visit www.buhrmasterfarms.com for more CSA information.

Buhrmaster Farms has a full line of artisanal cheeses and bakery items — including pies, cakes, cookies as well as handmade fudge — and local and seasonal fresh fruits, flowers, shrubs and vegetables...

PICK YOUR OWN BERRIES

Buhrmaster Farms' "PICK YOUR OWN" **Strawberry Patch** is open from mid-June to July. "PICK YOUR OWN" **Blueberries** start in July — both located at the corner of Worden Rd and Swaggertown Rd, in Scotia NY, 12302. *Compost and mulch are available now!* ADV.

Buhrmaster Farms
189 Saratoga Road (Route 50)
Scotia, NY 12302
(518) 399-5931
www.buhrmasterfarms.com

Nicole Squadere of *Lil Rita's Café* grew up working at her parents' *Publik House* in Malta. After graduating with a degree in English, she moved to Boston, Massachusetts, where she worked as a bartender for 10 years. After a two-year stint in Tuscon, Arizona, her aunt, Rita became hospitalized here. Nicole moved to Schenectady, and later opened **Lil Rita's Café** in honor of her late aunt… Nicole aka "Lil Rita" offers a full menu of eclectic entrées and specialty drinks that she makes — as well as handmade home decor that she crafts in the basement of the café. **Lil Rita's Café**
432 Franklin St • Schenectady, NY 12305

(518) 348-9536

ARTISAN • FOOD • DECOR